DEDICATION

This book is dedicated to my father Herzl, who used to carry a book of poems that I was featured in with him in his briefcase to show his friends and colleagues. He always supported me with my crazy adventures and creative ventures and is looking down on me from heaven chuckling over this book and my obsession with animals.

This book is also dedicated to my 2-legged support systems - Andrew, Brian, Brittin, Caroline, Charmaine, David, David, Donna, Doug, Elizabeth, Ellen, Grace, Jeff, Jillie, Lateace, Marcia, Maria, Matt, Peter, Ric, and Steve and to all the sentient 4-legged friends we love, especially my current family Marlon Brandog, Stella, Hope, and Max-A-Million-Kisses.

This book is also dedicated to all of the rescue groups who have strength of heart and soul to face the worst side of humanity to save, nurture and give better lives to animals who need our help as much as we need theirs.

Illustrations © 2025 by Eli Ziv

Published by Vivie Publishing

ISBN: 979-8-9903120-0-5

Library of Congress Control Number: 2024913305

Printed in United States

First Edition

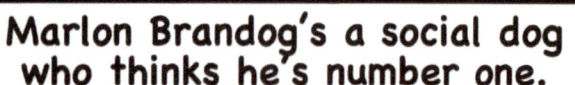

Marlon Brandog's a social dog who thinks he's number one.

I'm so Awesome!

Stella's a one-womog dog who won't play with others for fun.

Don't you even think about it!

Max-a-million-kisses always living up to his name.

I love you-so love you!

Being independent is Hope's way of playing the game.

I love my space... I'm so comfy...

Stella is Marlon Brandog's twin, who loves running after creatures.

Squirrel!

Bird!

She's a pretty, shy girl; her doe eyes her best features.

Is it ok to come out?

She taps her womog on the shin when she wants to go out,

LET ME FINISH!

TAP! TAP!

Mom, I want to go out!

And leaves her hair in every place she has been and gone about.

I'm thirsty, I'm going to get water!

Max-A-Million-Kisses is forever the baby of the ball.
He had a rough beginning, and he is healing from it all.
Someone please help me! I'm so scared!
ANIMAL SHELTER
YOU'RE OK NOW.
I'M GOING TO TAKE GOOD CARE OF YOU...
You feel so warm...
To help him recover, womog treats him like a king.
With the extra care, support, and love he can now dance and sing.
Oh, Seaweed!
I LOVE HOW MUCH FUN YOU GUYS HAVE AT THE BEACH!
Tag, you're It!
Who Is it?
Tag, I'm it!
I love my life!

Although they want to leave and get out in fresh air,
Womog grabs for the leashes and they all disappear.

TIME FOR WALKIES!

Marlon Brandog | Stella | Hope | Max

I'd hide but I really gotta go...

I have to make...but I love to hide.

"Let the games begin now!" they all bark to each other,
While one hides in the couch and one under the covers.

Come find me.

She'll never find me here.

A womog is patient as she walks with her band.
She must be because she has come to understand,

That each dog has its own way of doing its business.
Only then can they speed up to walk for their fitness.

Each dog has their own special morning routine
To get their day started—you know what I mean.

Who was here?

Who was here?

Our detective dog sniffs every single tree and blade of grass,
Investigating the scent of any other dogs that have passed.

Now all the other dogs will know that I've been here!

-10-

A second dog is on squirrel duty, waiting to chase,
Tugging the womog all over the place.

A third spins eighty times as he goes 'round and 'round
And makes himself dizzy before finally squatting down.

When one dog stops walking because he feels bushed,
Into the stroller he goes to be pushed.

Mom, I'm done walking NOW.

Pick me up, pick me up, pick me up

One would think that such a sight must look absurd,
But the stares the womog gets mean nothing to her.

GOOD MORNING!

I am King!

WHAT'S WITH DOGS IN STROLLERS?

SMH

A womog loves everything about her four-legged children.
To her their breath and their paws smell like freshly washed linen.

And a womog always knows which of her kids has been bad,
A guilty look on their face as they walk away sad.

Each dog, says the womog, has its own way of being,
Of letting her know what they feel and are thinking.
STELLA!!! COME HERE. STELLA!!! STELLA!?!?!?
Pet me! Pet me!
I am King!
Nope, nope!
I love my space!
Some are shy, some are lazy, some feisty and bold,
And some of them never do what they're told.

A womog always feels safe and sound with her brood,
Knowing what's going on in her neighborhood.

Whether car door, pedestrian, or small foreign sound,
The dogs are hyper alert to what's all around.

"Hey, Mom" they say as they bark and act tough.
"We got your back. No need to worry about stuff."

When the womog has visitors, each dog checks them out,
Barking and sniffing all who come in with their snout.

They stay by her side while she earns her living.
Supporting her space is their way of giving.

—18—

But when they get bored and need more attention
Her dogs get in her face with a clear-cut intention.

They nuzzle and poke her and give her sad eyes
Until she finally agrees to set her own work aside.

Bath time for a womog is always a pain.
It's a wonder washing her dogs doesn't drive her insane.

BATH TIME!

I'll pray For you...

The torture Begins...

No!!!

Better you Than me!

They wiggle and struggle, four paws in the air,
As she tries to work shampoo into their hair.

I'm out of here!

I'm out of here!

I'm out of here!

I WILL NEVER UNDERSTAND WHY YOU GET LIKE THIS OVER A BATH...

Help! Help!

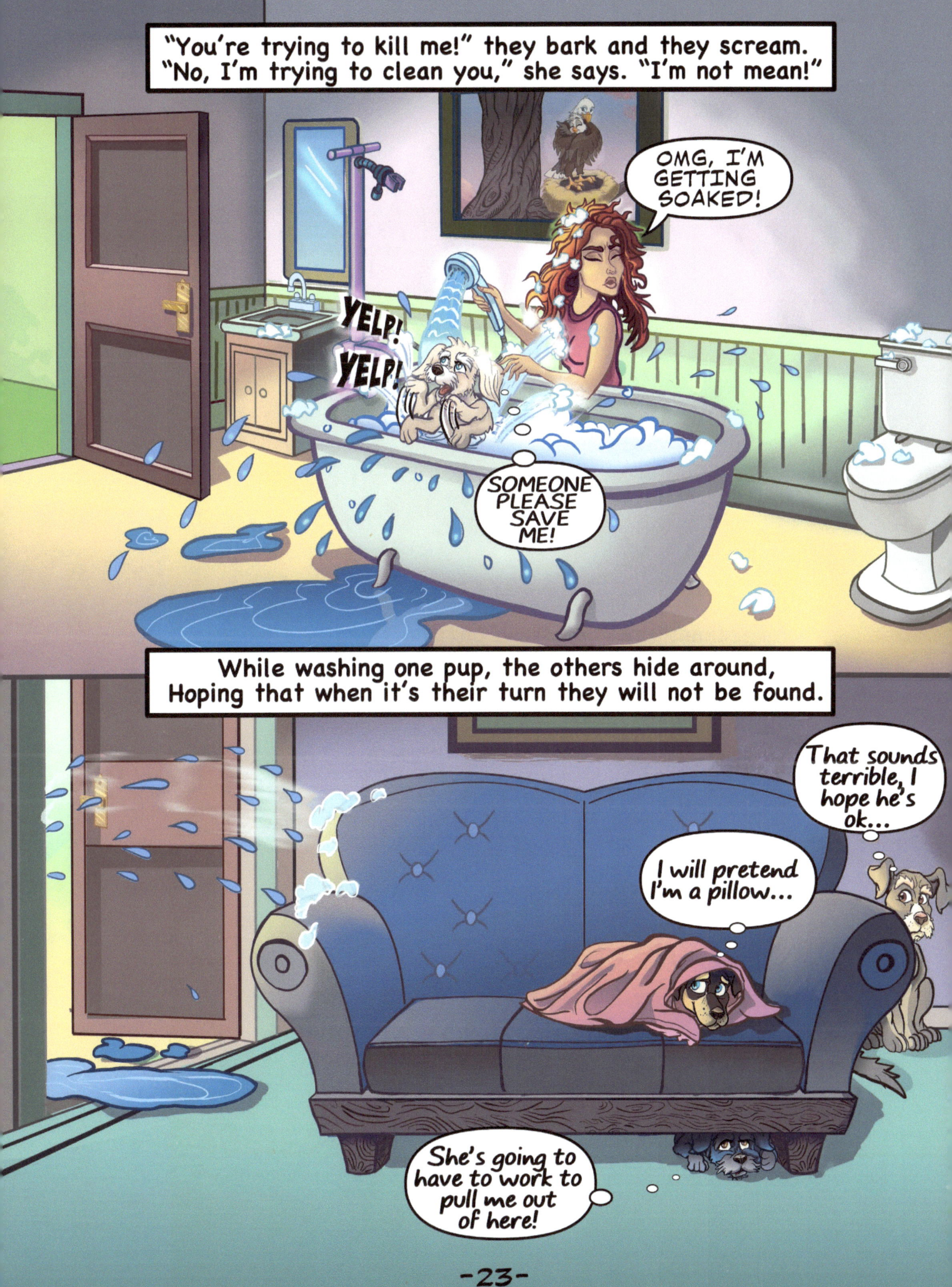

"You're trying to kill me!" they bark and they scream.
"No, I'm trying to clean you," she says. "I'm not mean!"

OMG, I'M GETTING SOAKED!

YELP!

YELP!

SOMEONE PLEASE SAVE ME!

While washing one pup, the others hide around,
Hoping that when it's their turn they will not be found.

That sounds terrible, I hope he's ok...

I will pretend I'm a pillow...

She's going to have to work to pull me out of here!

-23-

They're patient while she brushes their teeth to look bling,
But clipping their nails is a whole 'nother thing.

Peanut butter flavor!

Ooo, peanut butter, peanut butter...

I hope she will get that piece that is stuck in my back tooth...

She did a great job!

Sometimes she resorts to putting them in a muzzle
To get her dogs to stop their unrelenting struggle.

WOULD YOU CALM DOWN! I'M JUST TRYING TO CLIP YOUR NAILS...

Nope Nope Nope!

I WILL BE DONE IN A MINUTE...

That was a dirty Trick!

Once they are clean and as well-groomed as can be,
They roll on the floor and zoom back and forth with glee.
I feel so pretty!
Thanks Mom!
I am King again!
I smell so fresh!
"Thank you!" they say with their eyes and their smile.
"I know dealing with me sometimes takes a while."

When holidays with fireworks displays come around
The womog's household hunkers down.

Her scared balls of fur stay close to their mom,
With incense and soft music keeping them calm.

A womog's top priority is the health of her pet.
Whenever they're sick, she takes them straight to the vet.
My tummy hurts...

At any time of day or night and in any kind of weather,
A womog will pay a hefty fee to make her babies better.
DO YOU HAVE A PAYMENT PLAN?
I shouldn't have eaten that plant!

When a womog is feeling under the weather
Her crew stay by her side until she gets better.

They lie all around her and try not to worry,
Kissing and watching over her to heal in a hurry.

At the end of the day, it's time for a cuddle.
They head for the bed, where they all get to snuggle.

One on her leg, one spooning, and one by her head,
While another prefers the floor next to her instead.

It's a time to feel the love they pour into her heart,
The love that gives the womog's dreams a good start.

She scratches each one with a different appendage
To make sure they all get love with equal percentage.

It may be a sacrifice for her own comfortability,
And it definitely tests her own agility-

But a Womog would not have it any other way.
"A dogs place is on the bed" she will always say.

A womog will stay by her dogs until the very end
"Thank you for everything and for being my best friend-"

Welcome...

I WILL NEVER FORGET YOU OR STOP LOVING YOU!!!

Please take care of our womog!

I'm feeling tired...

We promise we will take care of her down here...

Safe journey!

I wonder if there are squirrels where you're going... Let me know...

"I know your doggie lifeline isn't as long as mine,
But the time that I have spent with you has truly been divine".

A day in the life of a womog is grand,
But unless you have dogs you may not understand.
I LOVE YOU GUYS...
We love you mom!
We love you mom!
And for all of the pain in the arse that they are,
The love that they give back outweighs it by far.
The End

About the Illustrator

Eli Ziv is a professional illustrator and graphic designer. He's currently working on projects with The Teabook and Caffeine & Ink. Eli studied art and animation at the Academy of Entertainment Technology in Los Angeles. He has worked for Angeleno artist "Kai" as a concept artist and for Red Phoenix Books as a children's book illustrator. Eli grew up as the child of Russian immigrants in Israel. He loved watching Saturday morning cartoons, which influenced him to become an artist. His other influences include mythology, classic literature, world history, space, fantasy and his wild imagination. You can see his graphic works at www.elizivart.com